Be Your Personal Best

CONFIDENCE

CHRISTOPHER RAPPOLD

Mr. Media Books

Be Your Personal Best: Confidence
(c) 2016 by Christopher M. Rappold

ISBN-13: 978-1530825967

ISBN-10: 1530825962

Published by Mr. Media Books, St. Petersburg, Florida

For information, contact the author:
founder@personalbestkarate.com

To order additional print copies of Be Your Personal Best Confidence — please visit http://www.MrMediaBooks.com

Front and Back Cover Design by Lori Parsells
http://www.VibranceAndVision.com

FOR ALL THE TEACHERS, MENTORS AND FRIENDS WHO HAVE GRACIOUSLY CONTRIBUTED THEIR TIME AND EXPERIENCES TO HELPING ME UNDERSTAND MY OWN SELF-CONFIDENCE, I OFFER THIS BOOK AS A COLLECTION OF YOUR THOUGHTS MIXED WITH MY OWN PERSPECTIVE AS A WAY OF PAYING IT FORWARD.

CONTENTS

"Believe in yourself!
Have faith in your abilities!
Without a humble but reasonable confidence
in your own powers
you cannot be successful or happy."
Norman Vincent Peale

INTRODUCTION
WHY CONFIDENCE?

The realization that you can help your child discover his or her Personal Best is very empowering. As parents, we want to provide the very best we can for our children. When a child is born, everything is perfect. The slate is clean and the anticipation of their potential is unlimited. We have dreams of their future and who they are going to become. We want for them to experience a life better than what we had.

Then, our hopes and dreams for our children run into daily life. We realize that, like us, our children have fears, doubts and worries. They have unanticipated insecurities that we never had, and mirror some of the same insecurities we have struggled with our whole life. They come face-to-face with a world through television, movies, social media and peer example that messages them 24/7 the opposite of what we have told them. As a result of mixed messages, what arises is questioning structure and belief in themselves. Images of who and what is "in" and "cool" and what is not becomes a tension in the back of their mind. Suddenly, we realize we are in a battle against the thousands of messages of input and their own shortcomings, and it's a battle we can't afford to lose.

With all this going against us, how can we insure that our children live the life we truly believe they are capable of? This book is a compilation of best practices from child psychology, personal development and the best of what we believe and reinforce every day in our character based martial arts program to help increase confidence.

It is confidence that will help them stay true to themselves, stay true to their beliefs. It is confidence that will help them follow their dreams and be happy in life. And this is what we want for our children.

Perhaps we need to lead by example; perhaps we need to make sure we are exemplifying the qualities our children need to see in order for them to gain confidence on their own. In the pages that follow are great reminders for us to instill the self-confidence we need to be successful in our own lives as well.

Take the ideas and start to implement them into your approach and communication with your children. By staying the course you can enjoy the confidence of knowing you are providing the very best guidance and support to assist them in their journey of realizing their full potential.

All the Best,
Christopher Rappold
5-Time World Karate Champion
Founder
Personal Best Karate
Child Safety Consultant
Norton, Massachusetts

con·fi·dence

noun

the feeling or belief that one can rely on someone or something; firm trust.

synonyms: trust, belief, faith, credence, conviction

the state of feeling certain about the truth of something.
a feeling of self-assurance arising from one's appreciation of one's own abilities or qualities.

1. CONFIDENCE DEFINED

What is confidence? The more definitions we have when defining a word like confidence, the better our total understanding will be.

Confidence can be defined as a belief in oneself and one's power or abilities, a self -reliance or self-assurance. Confidence is a person's ability to feel optimistic about something he has not done before. Confidence is a feeling that you can do something well or succeed at something.

However you choose to define it, most would agree a lack of confidence will stifle potential.

"Think you can, think you can't
– either way you are right."

Henry Ford

2. CONFIDENCE IS A PROCESS, NOT A DESTINATION

Having realistic expectations is important. Confidence is a state of mind that has a natural and normal ebb and flow to it. No one walks through life being 100% self-confident at all times. Environments, circumstance and situations change. And with each new place we find ourselves in, self-confidence may shift.

The first goal offered is to be in control enough so that we are able to perform in any situation at or above our expertise. For example, self-confidence will not help you on a test you didn't adequately prepare for, but it will help you to feel at your best to have the recall needed to answer the questions correctly. Confidence will not help you hit a baseball if you don't know how to swing a bat, but it will give you the ability to step up and try. Confidence will not make you immune to voices of criticism, but it will help you to keep your inner voice louder than the critics.

Goal number two; be a peace with the understanding that you cannot and will not be great at everything and loved by everybody. It is perfectly normal to have great confidence in one area of your life and have less confidence in another. People who are the best in one area of their life are often that good because they spend a disproportionate amount of time in that one area which by default will create deficiencies in other areas. Take comfort in knowing that if you truly have the desire to have more expertise in another area of your life, confidence will get you to start and repetition will grow your skills set. With an increase in skill, set your confidence in that area will rise. Practice increases confidence.

Whether someone likes you or not often comes from their own issues and perceptions that you may have little control over. Have you ever heard someone say, "That person reminds me of...." or "I just don't like that person." Sometimes it could be jealousy or other issues that extend deep into that person's past. The point is, why zap your energy worrying about something that is so distance and out of your control? Instead, keep your focus on being the best YOU can be by giving positive energy in as many interactions as possible. Take comfort in knowing there has never been a person, since the beginning of time, who has walked this planet and was loved by everyone. Keep your internal voice supportive, strong and positive and know you will be enough.

"It's not how you do compared to anyone else. It's how you do compared to how you could have done with all the skills and abilities that have been given to you. Keep your total focus on the development of being the best you, you can be."

Chris Rappold

3. PERSONAL BEST THINKING FOR PRESENT PROGRESS

The hallmark of Personal Best thinking is a total focus on your personal progress when compared to how you have done in the past. The past may be yesterday, two weeks ago, a month or year ago. Whatever you choose to use matters less. What is important is that you resist the temptation to compare yourself with others.

Why is this important? Most of the time the comparison with others is like comparing apples to oranges. Think about it - you get the highest score in the class on your Spanish test, you feel great right? Well, you shouldn't feel that great because you were already speaking the language coming into the class, therefore you should be always outperforming everyone. Think about it – you are working out and just completed 25 straight push-ups and you feel great. Last month your highest was 18. Unfortunately the feeling passes when you look over your shoulder and catch someone in the gym you have never met before doing sets of one handed push-ups. Immediately your motivation dwindles and you feel weak again.

The common challenge is that we live in a comparison based

society and it is far more common to measure against others than it is against yourself. Break from the norm and allow your feelings of progress to be based solely on doing better than before and watch what this does to empower your feelings of motivation and confidence. It immediately puts you in the driver's seat of how you feel.

"We may be personally defeated,

but our principles -- never!"

William Lloyd Garrison

4. LIVE BY YOUR PRINCIPLES

Principles are those fundamental truths in life that form the basis for you being the very best and most confident version of you. As true and predictable as gravity, they help to guide and shape the way you see the world and go through life. Life is filled with distractions and changes in life circumstances. Principles however, never change. They bind you to the ground and keep you centered. Though sometimes principles are ignored, they are ever present.

For example, if one of your principles in life is share respect to all then that is what you do. You are not forced to, but if you choose not to give respect to someone you will suffer the negative consequences of that choice. Just like holding a ball over your head, if you choose not to respect the principle of gravity and let the ball go you will inevitably experience the ball hitting your head.

Getting clear on what your principles in life are provides for you a roadmap for living. If you pick as your principles to live by respect, courtesy, honesty, self-control, self-discipline and, of course, confidence you start to ask yourself, " if these are the principles I am committed to living my life by, what would I have to do today, or this week, or in this situation to honor the principles that are important to me. And just like a magnet you will find yourself drawn to making decisions that represent you holding true to the principles and enjoying the accompanying results.

"When there is faith and clarity in the future there is power in the present."

Zig Ziglar

5. GET CRYSTAL CLEAR

It is awesome when a child shares their hopes and dreams about what they will do when they are all grown up. It doesn't matter what the vision is or how far-fetched you may believe their ideals are; it is simply a worthy gift to be able to dream about a bright future. This can be a source of self-confidence, as they envision their life and what they want in the future.

Often what can be built upon a conversation with a child about their vision for their future are additional follow-up questions clarify their goals. Questions like: "How do you think your life will be different when have reached your goal?", "How do you think you will feel?", "How old will you be when you reach this goal?", "Who will your friends be?", "What kind of car, house, vacations, etc. will be in your life?" , "What kind of person will you be --generous, kind, patient, confident, etc.?" ,"What kind of health will you have?", "What do you think your hobbies will be?" and "How will you spend your time?"

The idea is to use the creativity as an opportunity to expand their dream and bring clarity to it. The more clear the dream is, the more real it will feel. The more real it will feel, the more likely they are to stay motivated to pursue it. If they are clear on their goals it will help them stay confident through their days that what they are striving for can actually happen.

A great exercise to do with your child is to have them create a vision board for what their future will look like. A vision board is a visual representation of what their future will look like. It can be drawn or done by cutting out pictures from magazines and fixing them to a poster board. When complete, the vision board represents a continual reminder of what their future will look like. Displaying it on the wall where they can regularly see it is a great way to keep them engaged in the process of crystalizing their future.

"If we take care of the moments,
the years will take care of themselves."

Maria Edgeworth

6. SETTING BIG PROGRESS MARKERS —SMALL IS THE NEW BIG

Goal setting seems to be a given in being able to measure progress; however, when looking to build confidence it is perhaps even more important to keep yourself on the path to the person you are capable of becoming.

For our purposes, I am going to suggest some tweaks to the typical body of work that is associated with goal setting. For starters, I am going to encourage you to break down your victories into the smallest possible chunks of progress. The steps forward will almost be unrecognizable to on lookers, but over time your progress will be noticed by all. Let me explain.

Let's imagine you pick a confidence goal of standing up to someone who intimidates you. Rather than labeling yourself a success when you muster the courage to tell this person how you feel, you are going to break down the forward progress in as small a progression as possible. Maybe the first place you are going to start is by monitoring your breathing when you are around the person. Make sure you are taking a few deep breaths when you are around this person.

When you see and feel your self-confidence grow it is very reinforcing and motivating. It will find yourself thinking and acting in more empowering ways.

"We meet aliens every day who have something to give us. They come in the form of people with different opinions."

William Shatner

7. DON'T MAKE YOUR SELF-WORTH CONDITIONAL ON BEING VALIDATED BY OTHERS

Everyone enjoys the compliments and validation from each other that you are doing a great job. It is normal and natural. Many times, though, especially as you are making progress, there may not be someone right there to tell you that you are doing well. There are other situations where you work really hard on a project to get it complete and when you finally show it to others, it is met with a lukewarm response. Immediately you feel under-appreciated or start to question whether it was as good as you originally thought.

The remedy for this is to set your own criteria for what a good job is and give yourself the internal credit for progress made. Know that for reasons beyond your control the response you get from others could be factors that have nothing to do with you (someone is not feeling well, they are preoccupied with other thoughts, they are dealing with other pressing issues, they are simply processing it all in, etc.)

By assuming the worst you immediately deflate yourself.

By validating yourself and not depending on it to come from others, when receiving an acknowledgement you can use it as an additional pat on the back. If it doesn't come, it wasn't needed anyways.

Focus on doing the task or assignment to your standard of excellence and know that this is enough.

"I don't know. Just because someone's pretty

doesn't mean she's decent. Or vice versa.

I'm not into appearances. I like flaws,

I think they make things interesting."

Sarah Dessen, The Truth About Forever

8. CHANGE YOUR BODY LANGUAGE AND IMAGE

A powerful influencer over the way we feel is how we choose to use our body. Remember being told as a strategy to "Take a deep breath" or "Go take a walk", what you probably found, if you followed the advice, was it actually worked!

I remember sitting in a classroom in grade school when all of a sudden the principal walked into the room. Immediately everyone in class sat up straight and tall and miraculously had A+ focus and energy.

I also remember the feeling of walking through a haunted house and having monsters unexpectedly jump out at me. By the time I made it through, the last thing on my mind was feeling tired.

Each one of these examples illustrates the power of using your physiology (body) and physiognomy (face) to create feelings in your mind. If this is true and you can access how you feel on the inside by changing what you do on the outside, then let's use this to our advantage.

Here are some simple things that can be done to on the outside to change the way you feel on the inside:

Exercise – Putting aside all of the health benefits that are life-lasting, consistent daily exercise that gets your body moving may be the very best way to shake yourself up every day so you can be the very best version on you. Contrary to what some think, exercise doesn't take energy. There is no excuse of "I'm too tired to exercise". It actually creates a mental and physical high that will elevate your performance throughout the day.

Smile – In life we have a choice to be an energy giver, or an energy taker. The doorway to this decision is the look on your face. Just the act of having a pleasant welcoming look on your face emits to the people around you positive energy. The simple habit of smiling alone has been shown to completely change someone's outlook over time. It is very powerful if used. Start today to turn that frown upside down and notice the difference in how you feel and how the world interacts with you.

Act - One of the talents I have great admiration for is acting. I am so impressed when an actor can fully immerse himself into a role, enough for me as the viewer to forget they are just playing a role. I think we can take a lesson from this art. Modeling the way a confident person would walk, talk, breath, gesture, etc. is a way to shortcut feeling confident. Start to notice people in your surroundings who exhibit the level of confidence you want to feel and start as an actor does to mimic what you see. At first it is normal and natural to feel a little awkward at first, but just like the actor who practices his lines, it will become more and more natural.

Put on the finishing touches – I remember reading about a behavioral study that was conducted using dress down days and dress up days at school. There was a correlation between dress down days and a higher incidence of poor behavior. Conversely, there was also a correlation found in better behavior when the children came to school wearing formal clothing, such as dresses and ties. What's the take away? How you look on the outside can positively affect the way you feel. Knowing this, it stands to reason that to put your best foot forward and make certain that when you need to be performing at a high level that you are well-groomed and dressed for success. This is not being superficial; it is merely piecing together the outfit (outside) to match the character (inside) you want to have. Remember, it is your choice. Take the time to package yourself for the outcome you want.

"One important key to success is self-confidence. An important key to self-confidence is preparation."

Arthur Ashe

9. BE PREPARED

There is a saying that success happens when preparation meets opportunity. In my experience this is true. Being adequately prepared for what is going to happen heightens your ability to act in a confident manner.

Each time when I was preparing myself to compete for the world karate championship I took the time to think through every scenario that could happen in the ring. I pictured having the lead. I pictured being down one point. I pictured the audience cheering for me and cheering against me. I imagined time was running out and I was able to stay calm and do what needed to be done to become victorious. Every scenario that I could possibly think of was used to ensure when it was time to step in the ring and do it for real, that I would feel on the inside and project on the outside a feeling of complete and total confidence.

Now let's bring it off sports and use the same strategy for planning out a week. There is an optimum cycle of preparedness that can happen each and every week. By following the system it always keeps you out in front of the obligations you will have.

It starts on Sunday with a seven day view of your upcoming week. Take the time to write down and think through all of the commitments you have for the week ahead. This should include school work, tests, one-on-one meetings, social gatherings, family activities etc. Put it in front of you on a sheet of paper or using a program that allows you to see the whole week at a glance. Next, take the time to anticipate what might go wrong, what may take longer than expected, who or what may give you a level of resistance. Factor in additional time or think through everything from best case to worst case scenarios.

Prepare like a pro athlete in making sure everything is thought through so that whatever comes up, you are ahead of the curve and already have a plan and a response. Maybe you have heard this expression: "Plan for the worst, hope for the best." I would add on, "Be prepared for whatever happens." Positive thinking is great, but for who never take the time to consider not getting the result they want are setting themselves up for a feeling of failure or continuous disappointment.

You alone are responsible for your preparation. Invest the time and watch your confidence sore.

"The best vitamin for making friends? B1!"

Author Unknown

10. GIVING IS ENERGY GIVING

For some, to make a friend takes time, effort and energy. Thinking about this is can be a daunting task. An effortless way to get around what you may perceive as an energy drain is to be a giver. What do I mean? It takes mental effort when meeting someone to craft a way for you to be interesting to the person you are meeting. You ask yourself, "How do I act?" and "What do I say?" all the while feeling stress on the inside.

Instead of taking that approach, how about focusing on being more interested than interesting? Take the spotlight off yourself and sincerely be interested and curious about who they are, what they do and how you can help them. From their perspective it will be so refreshing to meet a person who is not trying to make themselves look good, but rather is interested in them.

If you think about it, creating a relationship is based on the person, liking, trusting and respecting you. What better way to facilitate this happening than to unselfishly allow them the spotlight to share what they want about themselves with you.

I was taking a two hour plane flight a few years ago and by chance I was seated next to a gentleman who was wearing a bowler's jacket. I commented on the jacket and his eyes lit up. Taking the cue I then asked him a question about how long he has been bowling, will he be competing in a tournament in the near future, and so on. Well, two hours later when the wheels hit the ground the conversation ended. As the gentleman deplaned to head out to his bowling tournament he turned to me and said, "I really enjoyed our conversation and getting to know you." The reality is though he never asked me anything about me. For two hours, I kept the conversation on him, as a result, he felt connected enough to me that he felt he made a friend. That's one real life example of this approach in action.

When you give sincere interest to another, you leapfrog over all the other people who will only be trying show how important they are. Take the time to show interest in that person first and you will have the opportunity to fast track your relationship. Then when the conversation does swing to what you do, the person will want to give you their full and undivided attention. Giving the spotlight is energy giving to the person, but also immensely energy giving back to yourself.

Change the focus from you to the person you are meeting. Instead of thinking about what you can get, think about what you can give. You can never go wrong with this approach to making human connections.

"Happiness cannot be traveled to, owned, earned, worn or consumed. Happiness is the spiritual experience of living every minute with love, grace, and gratitude."

Denis Waitley

11. THE ANTIDOTE FOR A LACK OF CONFIDENCE—A GRATITUDE LIST

Lacking self-confidence is a focus on not being enough. Coming from this feeling, it is no wonder it feels hard to get out of your own way. The good news is there is a way you can take control of this feeling of not having enough. It starts with a simple inventor of what you have. Think about it: how much would someone have paid 20 years ago for the phone you carry in your pocket today? How much would someone in 1995 have paid for the total and complete access you have to the internet today? How much would a person have paid who died of a disease that today has a cure? The answer to each of these questions is so big that it can't be defined. The challenge is because we are so close to what we have, we tend to take it for granted. By taking the time to read through and continually add to all the things you have in your life that you are grateful for, instead of coming from a place of lack you start to change your feeling to coming from a place of abundance.

Start with the obvious and grow your list. Food, and not just food, but the variety of food that wasn't even available ten years ago. Clothing but not just nice clothing but the choices of stores and styles that didn't exist prior to this time. And there's also shelter - do you realize in your community right now there are people who do not have a warm place to sleep in the winter or a cool place in the summer?

Start with these and be on the lookout each day for the big things (food, clothing and shelter) and the small things (the person who let you pull out in traffic or the person who smiled at you) you appreciate.

A great way to stay in touch and in tune with this is to be of service to others. Join a movement or a service organization that provides something of value to those less fortunate. It will keep your feet on the ground and provide a continual reminder of all the things to be grateful for.

"Good timber does not grow with ease, the stronger the wind, the stronger the trees"

Malloch

12. ACKNOWLEDGE AND WELCOME ALL OF YOUR EXPERIENCES

You is it! I know that's bad grammar, but it is true. The mix of favorites and not so favorites, the good and the bad, the strengths and the weaknesses -- all add up to form who you are today. The exciting part about being human is that most things can be changed or improved.

Allow me to move to an analogy to illustrate the point I want to make. Let's imagine you are carrying a piece of furniture down a narrow hallway. As you navigate the turn into a room you misjudge and catch your finger in between the furniture and the wall…Ouch. Has it ever happened to you? Well it's happened to me and it hurts.

After you put the furniture down, you run your finger under cold water and apply some ice. Your finger at that moment isn't as good and functional as the other fingers but you take care of it and nurse it back to normal health.

Question, do you waste your time hating your finger, wishing it didn't exist, hoping your finger would just go away? Of course not.

You realize your bruised finger is as much a part of you as any other part of you. You know you are better with it than without it, so you do what you can to nurse it back to full health and function.

Each part of you --your fears, doubts and worries, anxieties and things you perceive as imperfections-- are all in the mix of what makes you who you are. If you perceive any of them bruised or in need of improvement or repair, then simply attend to them with the same loving care you would give to a hurt finger. Take the time to determine what needs to happen to make whatever part of you needing healing or improvement better. Hating a part of yourself is as helpful as hating your finger for getting hurt, it's wasted energy that could be invested in other ways to make you.

Human beings are imbued with the choice and the abilities to change virtually anything about themselves they want.

Recognizing this amazing freedom and taking small actions each day to move in the direction of the person you want to become may be the greatest secret to bringing your greatness to the surface getting your heart mind and soul to smile.

"You cannot expect to live a positive life if you hang with negative people."

Joel Osteen

13. STAY AWAY FROM NEGATIVE PEOPLE

I have always loved the analogy of the garden for teaching simple life lessons. One of the lessons that can be observed from the discipline of gardening is tending quickly to the inevitable weeds that will pop up and attempt to overtake your garden. If you have the opportunity to observe an experienced gardener you will see that when they see a weed pop up they will immediately pull it out of the ground and discard it. Gardeners know that lack of tending to weeds will shrink the potential of the harvest.

In life, we have the same experiences and challenges gardeners have only instead of pulling out the weeds our task is eliminating or significantly limiting time with people who do not have your best interest at stake. A good indicator to use in figuring out who is good for you and adds energy to your life is, how you feel about yourself when you are around a person. If the answer is "I feel better about myself when I am around this person", then that is a person to be around. If you answer this question honestly and you find the answer is, "I don't feel very good about myself" or "I find I am second guessing my abilities a lot more" then it is in your best interest to limit or completely eliminate them from your circle of friends. When I say this, I don't mean in a cruel or disrespectful way, I simply mean for your own sake you need to move away from the relationship.

Finding and surrounding yourself with people in your life who encourage, support, believe and see more in you than you do in yourself creates a life that is both fun and enjoyable to live in. Having people in your life that are the opposite slowly erode your confidence and cause you to question things that need not be focused on. Give yourself the gift of an uplifting peer network and watch your life soar to greatness.

"To the degree we're not living our dreams,
our comfort zone has more control of us
than we have over ourselves."

Peter McWilliams

14. STEP OUT OF YOUR COMFORT ZONE AT SOCIAL EVENTS

If you are like over half the population, the idea of going to an unfamiliar social event can make you feel nauseous. Enjoying the company of friends is one thing, but being at an event where you may not know anyone is simply, in your mind, no fun. You wonder how you are going to deal with meeting people; what should you wear, what image do you want to portray and how will you make yourself interesting to others.

Recognize this event as an opportunity for self-expansion. The best way to attack this event is to commit with courage to be the first: the first one to say, "Hi" to people, the first one to give a compliment, the first one to share a smile or an approving look, the first one to offer someone a chair or some assistance. Playing small and being in the background will only feed the feeling of being uncomfortable. Instead of this, notice how many opportunities there are for you to be the first.

One of the surprising things you will find as well is how many other people attending the event were feeling the same way you felt. Seek these people out and commit to extending a hand a friendship to them. Be as kind and generous as you can. By keeping you focus on this and your place in being first, I think you will find your experience will be transformed.

"What comes easy won't last,
what lasts won't come easy"
Author Unknown

15. AVOID GIVING IN TO IMMEDIATE GRATIFICATION—IT OFTEN LEADS TO SELLING YOURSELF SHORT

The mirage of immediate gratification has stifled more individual progress than anything in history. I realize that is a pretty big statement and one not to be taken lightly.

Immediate gratification gives you instant short term release or good feelings, unfortunately it can keep you and your results small. Anything worthy of a second look requires a degree of sacrifice. Sometimes known as *patience*, deferring gratification allows the accumulation of something that will potentially have high-lasting value.

How does this apply to confidence? Immediate gratification mindset craves instant results. For example, you muster up the courage to say, "Hi" to someone and since you don't immediately get back an enthusiastic response you conclude your efforts are not working. This sets you back and prevents you from willingly continuing the habit of being friendly because you weren't immediately rewarded.

Avoid this short term thinking, invest in having some faith and stay to the course knowing that over time your continual efforts to build your confidence muscle will win out.

"Perfection itself is imperfection."

Vladimir Horowitz

16. LET ME SAVE YOU THE SUSPENSE... YOU ARE NOT PERFECT

Sound negative? Actually, it is a very positive message. When you come from a place where you realize you nor anyone else who has ever walked this world is perfect, then the pressure is off. You go out into the world knowing you are going to make mistakes just like everyone. You are going to say things and do things that you will regret. You are going to be as perfectly imperfect as anyone and that is OK. It puts you in great company with everyone else in the human race.

It is not negative to believe the previous paragraph; in fact, I would say to disagree with it is a form of delusion that creates a lot of unnecessary stress and anxiety in life. The greatest illusion in the world in the illusion of perfection. There is no such thing, the only perfect people we see are generally the people we don't know so well. Peeking behind the curtain on anyone will reveal many of the flaws we all are working through.

Too much time is wasted beating ourselves up over two things: regrets of mistakes of the past or needless worrying about the future. It's time to let this all go and focus simply and completely on one activity: Being the very best you that you can be each and every day. Self-confidence will rise and fears, doubts and worries will slowly but surely fall off.

A little boy was having difficulty

lifting a heavy stone.

His father came along just then.

Noting the boy's failure, he asked,

"Are you using all your strength?"

"Yes, I am," the little boy said impatiently.

"No, you are not," the father answered.

"I am right here just waiting, and you haven't

asked me to help you."

–Anonymous

17. ASK FOR HELP

It's sad but true. Many people equate asking for help as being less than. In some ways it makes them feel like they are somehow weak. In our culture we have tended to glorify the person who supposedly goes at it alone and takes on the world. The reality is ALL of us are dependent upon each other more than we realize and much more that is glorified often times on television in the movies.

Take sports, as an example. How good would Mia Hamm, Michael Jordan or Tom Brady be without their respective team members, coaches, trainer, mentors and supporting cast behind the scenes supporting them so their greatness could shine through? How about business - how good would Steve Jobs of Apple, Bill Gates of Microsoft or Mark Zuckerberg of Facebook be without the thousands of people who go to work every day to help fulfill their vision?

Save yourself a lifetime of confusion and lack of progress and simply accept that if you are no where you want to be or feel as confident as you want to feel then you need the help and support of people that can provide the correct direction and example for you.

18. FINAL THOUGHTS

Though obvious and often not given the attention it truly deserves, the gift of true self-confidence is the foundation that daily happiness and achievement are built upon. No matter the age or life experience, everyone can benefit from a tune-up or a tune into the potential unleashed when their self-confidence is allowed to shine.

What an amazing privilege it is to truly embrace and act on your ability to influence the growth and development of your child's full potential. By your example first and your gift of time and compassionate attention second, you will have the awesome ability to positively influence the direction and smooth journey your child's life will take. I stand with you as a resource, a fellow parent and a true believer in the awesome potential each one of us has within.

GET YOUR CHILD ON THEIR PERSONAL BEST PATH

Personal Best Karate is proud to offer self-confidence as a result of training with us. If you would give your child the gift of a FREE trial in our award winning character based martial arts program that will reinforce family value and teach mental and physical skills to ensure they are safe Please go to www.PersonalBestKarate.com.

We promise that our team of highly skilled martial arts teachers and mentors will help you and your family feel right at home.

ABOUT THE AUTHOR
CHRISTOPHER M. RAPPOLD

Christopher Rappold is a master teacher, trainer and blogger who has been working with children and families for more than 25 years. He has presented bullying programs to more than 30 school districts and is a widely recognized expert at presenting safety strategies and bullying prevention in layman's terms while also filling gaps left by educating and involving teachers, parents and school administrators.

Rappold is the founder of Personal Best Karate, martial arts schools presently located in New England, and serves as both an owner and president of the franchise. His form of teaching honors the potential of each student's individual capabilities and works to ensure just the right level of challenge is presented so that the student can maintain sustained and lasting growth and improvement.

Rappold has been a member of Team Paul Mitchell (the top-rated sport karate team in the world) dating back to 1988 and currently serves as the team's Executive Director. Rappold has also won the W.A.K.O. World Championship in three different weight divisions.

For more information on Personal Best Karate programs, or to gift yourself or someone you know with a free trial, please call (508) 285-5425 or email info@personalbestkarate.com.